SEE HOW I LOVE YOU

Other publications by Sr Elizabeth Obbard include:

Lamps of Fire, daily readings with St John of the Cross (DLT 1984);
Magnificat the Journey and the Song (DLT 1986); *La Madre*,
the Life and Spirituality of St Teresa of Avila (St Paul 1994);
Introducing Julian, Woman of Norwich (New City 1995);
The History and Spirituality of Walsingham (The Canterbury Press
Norwich 1995).

She has also contributed to various books and periodicals and
written and illustrated some books for children.

SEE HOW I LOVE YOU

*Meditating on the Way of the Cross
with Julian of Norwich*

ELIZABETH RUTH OBBARD, ODC

THE CANTERBURY PRESS
NORWICH

Text and line drawings © Sr Elizabeth Ruth Obbard ODC, 1996

First published 1996 by The Canterbury Press Norwich
(a publishing imprint of Hymns Ancient & Modern Limited,
a registered charity)
St Mary's Works, St Mary's Plain,
Norwich, Norfolk NR3 3BH

British Library Cataloguing in Publication Data

A catalogue record for this book is available
from the British Library

ISBN 1-85311-141-4

*Typeset by Chansitor Publications Ltd, Beccles, Suffolk
and printed in Great Britain by
The Lavenham Press
Lavenham, Suffolk*

FOR CAROLINE

ACKNOWLEDGEMENTS

My special thanks to Josef Pichler MHM for permission to use his own translation of Julian of Norwich's *Revelations of Divine Love*.

All Biblical quotations are from the NRSV. The New Revised Standard Version Bible, copyright 1989, Division of Christian Education of the National Council of the Churches of Christ in the United States of America, is published in London by Collins Publishers.

CONTENTS

Introduction   *page* 1

STATIONS

First   Jesus is condemned to death   13
Second   Jesus accepts the Cross   19
Third   Jesus falls the first time   25
Fourth   Jesus meets his Blessed Mother   31
Fifth   Simon of Cyrene helps Jesus carry the Cross   37
Sixth   Veronica wipes the face of Jesus   43
Seventh   Jesus falls the second time   49
Eighth   Jesus consoles the women of Jerusalem   55
Ninth   Jesus falls the third time   61
Tenth   Jesus is stripped of his garments   67
Eleventh   Jesus is nailed to the Cross   73
Twelfth   Jesus dies on the Cross   79
Thirteenth   Jesus is taken down from the Cross   85
Fourteenth   Jesus is laid in the Sepulchre   91

Epilogue   He is Risen, Alleluia   97

Index of Bible quotations   99

Index of Readings from *Revelations of Divine Love*   101

INTRODUCTION

Sometime around the year 1420 an old woman died in the anchorhold attached to St Julian's church in the Conisford district of Norwich. Her maid Sarah washed the body and laid it out in the little room.

The corpse was duly clothed in a coarse grey mantle with a white coif passing under the chin to hold the sparsely toothed jaws together. A crucifix was arranged between the cold fingers and the parish priest read the burial service over the dead woman for the second time in her life. Then the coffin was laid quietly to rest in an unmarked grave.

There were a number of mourners present: a smattering of relatives from a younger generation, paying their last respects to one who had been sequestered from ordinary family life for many years; but most were working folk from Conisford, a densely populated part of the city, who had revered this woman as a wise counsellor and had come to talk over their joys and sorrows with her while she lived.

For nigh on half a century this woman had dwelt in St Julian's anchorhold, meditating on a series of visions or 'Shewings' which she had received as a young woman of thirty. Shortly afterwards she had retired from active life and had herself enclosed in a small room that abutted the church. Indeed she had been identified with the place for so long that her ordinary name was now forgotten. She was known simply as the lady of St Julian's, which had contracted with time to 'the lady Julian'. She it is who has come down to posterity as Julian of Norwich—woman, Christian, mystic, one of the great spiritual theologians of medieval England.

From the brief biographical details that can be gleaned from Julian's writings she had been a pious young person, much given to prayer, which was hardly surprising considering the precariousness of life in the fourteenth century. The Hundred Years war was still in progress when she was born, and the dreaded plague had struck Norwich three times in her early years; first when she was seven years old and again at nineteen and twenty-five. Julian may have been married at some time, but the exterior circumstances of her life in childhood and youth can only be matters of conjecture. Presumably

1

she was a native of Norwich, a city that ranked second in importance to London, and was a thriving centre of trade and commerce. Its pride was its great cathedral dedicated to the Trinity, and the bustling streets of the city were thronged with friars, monks, priests, minstrels, tradesfolk, beggars, merchants and travellers from many lands, with housewives haggling over prices and trying to strike a good bargain. It was an enriching and stimulating place to live.

As a girl, Julian had prayed for three gifts: an experience of the Passion of Christ, a physical illness that would bring her to the verge of death at thirty years of age, and three wounds—the wound of contrition, the wound of kind (or natural) compassion, and the wound of unshakeable longing for God. She soon forgot her first two requests as she knew they were unusual, not things she had a right to ask for. That is why she says that she only asked for them conditionally, 'if God should want to give them'; but despite the passage of years they had obviously sunk deep into her subconscious mind. The third request for the wounds remained with her continually. In the wounds she was asking for gifts that, as a Christian, she felt she had every right to desire, and she had no qualms about making this request unconditionally.

Then when Julian was thirty and a half a severe illness prostrated her. It was May 1373 and her life was despaired of.

On May 8th, a priest was sent for to administer the Last Rites. By this time Julian was partially paralysed and unable to speak. The priest held the crucifix before the dying woman saying 'I have brought you the image of your Creator and Saviour. Look at it and let it comfort you'.

Julian, who had been gazing heavenward, forced herself to focus on the face of the crucified Christ. However, when she felt herself to be at the very point of death, her pain suddenly vanished and it came to her that, though she might well die, she should take this opportunity to ask for the second of her desired wounds—that of natural compassion for Christ in his sufferings.

> I wanted his pains to be my pains; to feel so deeply
> with him that I would long for God. But in this I never
> sought any bodily sight, nor any kind of vision from
> God, but rather the compassion that a soul could

> naturally have for our Lord Jesus, who out of love was willing to become a mortal man. So I desired to suffer with him while living in my mortal body, as God would give me grace. *(3:6)*

In other words, Julian desired to truly *feel*, physically and emotionally, something of the sufferings of Christ, just as anyone would experience anguish if they saw someone they loved in agony. An intellectual appreciation was not enough. Julian wanted her whole person to be involved, body, soul and spirit.

Even as Julian formulated her desire it seemed that the face of Christ on the cross before her came vividly to life. Her revelations, or 'Shewings' were beginning.

> And immediately I saw the red blood trickle down from under the garland of thorns; a living stream of hot, fresh blood, just as it was at the time of the passion when the crown of thorns was pressed on his blessed head. And I saw very clearly and powerfully that he, both God and man who suffered for me, was the very same one who showed this vision to me without any go-between.
>
> And in the same vision the Trinity suddenly filled my heart with the deepest joy. I immediately realised that this will be the permanent experience of those who go to heaven. For the Trinity is God. God is the Trinity. The Trinity is our maker, the Trinity is our keeper, the Trinity is our everlasting lover, the Trinity is our endless joy and bliss, through our Lord Jesus Christ and in our Lord Jesus Christ.
>
> And I said 'Benedicite Domine'. This I said out of reverence in a powerful voice, and I was absolutely overwhelmed with wonder and marvel to see that he who is so holy and so awesome should be so homely with a sinful creature living in this wretched flesh. *(4:1,2)*

While Julian watched, the sufferings of Jesus in his passion unfolded before her wondering eyes. It was a deeply personal experience, focused most especially on the face of Christ bowed beneath the crown of thorns.

Yet even in the midst of Christ's sufferings, Julian discovered what St John makes clear in his gospel—the passion was the moment of glory when the broken, mortal flesh of Jesus revealed uniquely the power and presence of the God of love.

That is why there is nothing morbid in Julian's writing. Everything is shot through with the joy of redemption accomplished. All is part of the great panorama of creation and salvation.

> During the whole time that I saw the head bleeding so heavily I could not stop saying these words 'Benedicite Domine'. In this vision I understood six things.
> The first is the work of his blessed passion and the shedding of so much of his precious blood.
> The second is the virgin who is his beloved mother.
> The third is the blessed Godhead who always was, is now, and shall be forever: almighty, all-wisdom, and all-love.
> The fourth is everything that he has made. For I saw quite well that heaven and earth and the whole of creation are great and vast, lovely and good. But the reason why everything seemed so small to me was because I saw everything in the presence of him who is the Creator. For to a soul that sees the Creator of all things, all that is created seems very little.
> The fifth is that he who created all things for love looks after everything out of the same love, now and forever.
> The sixth is that God is everything that is good, as I see it, and the goodness that everything has is God.
> All this our Lord showed me in the first revelation and he gave me space and time to contemplate it. Then the bodily vision ceased but the spiritual vision lived on in my understanding.
> In all this I was deeply moved with love for my fellow Christians, desiring that they too might all see and know the same that I had seen; for I wished it to be a comfort to them, because this vision was shown to me for all. *(8:1-3)*

4

Fifteen 'Shewings' followed one another in rapid succession, with a final Shewing after another crisis in Julian's illness a few days later.

Julian however did not die. She recovered and, sometime afterwards, when the anchorhold at St Julian's church fell vacant, chose to spend the rest of her life there meditating in solitude as she plumbed the depths and meaning of all she had seen in those few brief hours.

The vocation Julian embraced was not so very unusual in medieval England and was particularly popular in Norfolk. Norwich as a city had a strong hermit tradition, with several hermits mentioned in wills and an anchorhold at each city gate.

Any devout man or woman, lay or religious, could be accepted for the solitary life after mature reflection and a period of testing. If the vocation seemed genuine the burial service was read over the aspirant who then received a plain habit to wear as a sign of his or her consecration. Women were then enclosed in a small house, or even a single room, at the side of a church. From within, three windows (generally covered) communicated with the outside world. One window opened onto the church, where an anchoress could participate in the liturgy and receive communion; one faced the street, where people could come for comfort and counsel; while a third was for the use of a servant who liaised with tradespeople and thus ensured that her charge received the necessary material sustenance without having to leave her enclosure. Men were not usually so strictly confined; there were more options open as to where they lived and how they supported themselves. A number chose to live in the countryside as itinerant road or bridge repairers, or they might build a small hut and offer hospitality to travellers and pilgrims.

In her Norwich anchorhold Julian had many years in which to ponder her insights. Despite her revelations focusing on the passion everything she writes contains a note of deep joy and basic optimism. The cross became Julian's constant meditation, knowledge of Christ crucified her only wisdom. But beneath the blood and pain, intermingled with much homely imagery, there runs the thread of rejoicing. Julian acknowledges unambiguously the overpowering reality of the strength, both tender and reliable, residing in God's love; a love that endures forever and cannot, will not, be broken by sin on our part.

We cannot know for certain what kind of crucifix Julian contemplated, but two small bronze figures from processional crosses which may date from Julian's time are preserved in a small museum at the church of St Peter Hungate in Norwich. In these, Jesus' face is kind and naturalistic, the head bent graciously, the eyes open, with the blood from his wounds flowing onto his loincloth. The crown of thorns, which plays such a prominent part in Julian's vision, was just becoming popular in iconography. For her it was a highly symbolic circlet, not merely a crown of pain but a crown which held overtones of victory, kingship and triumphant rejoicing.

Julian's Shewings begin with the image of Christ crucified and from these work backward to the Incarnation and forward to the parousia. On this magnificent panorama she pondered for the remainder of her long life. But she also had to keep to a structured timetable that prescribed certain prayers to be said throughout the day; she had to earn her living as far as possible through sewing or other handwork, and be available for counselling. She would have been thoroughly integrated into the area of Conisford where she had her cell, and must have heard many a whispered confidence that could be shared with no one else. Margery Kempe, who visited Julian, found her a sympathetic listener and a wise woman, who gave Margery the gift of her time, whereas others were liable to dismiss her as a nuisance.

Julian did not know the devotion of the way of the cross in its present form. But she would certainly have been familiar with the ceremonies of Holy Week, maybe even 'creeping to the cross' in her youth hidden amidst the crowds gathered in the cathedral of the Holy Trinity. Also, every parish church had its Rood screen, with its great crucifix flanked by Our Lady and St John. In the contemporary Ancrene Riwle, a rule for anchoresses written for three women who shared an anchorhold near Salisbury, a Rule which was most likely followed at least in basic outline by Julian, we find a salutation of the cross to be recited daily in honour of the five wounds of Jesus as follows.

We adore you O Christ and we bless you,
because by your holy cross you have redeemed the world.
We adore your cross O Lord,
we commemorate your glorious passion.
Have mercy on us, you who suffered for us.
Hail O holy cross, worthy tree,
whose precious wood bore the ransom of the world.
Hail O cross, dedicated to the Body of Christ
and adorned with his limbs as with pearls.
O cross, victorious wood, true salvation of the world,
peerless among trees in leaf, flower and fruit.
Medicine of Christians,
save the sound and heal the sick.
Let what cannot be done by human power
be done in your name.   Amen.

The Way of the Cross was originally derived from the practice of pilgrims who were able to travel to Jerusalem and follow the path to Calvary in the actual city of Jesus' death and resurrection. Margery Kempe gives us a graphic account of her own pilgrimage to Jerusalem and the great impression made on her by seeing the holy places. Later the Franciscans, who had custody of the shrines in Palestine on behalf of the church, popularised a form of this devotion which made it possible for people to follow a 'way of the cross' without making the long and perilous journey to the Holy Land. They did this by erecting small crosses, fourteen was the final number agreed upon, which commemorated various 'stations' or stopping points, which marked events on Jesus' path to Calvary.

Around 1350, during Julian's lifetime, the Franciscans began erecting stations of the cross in Italy, and from there the devotion spread to other parts of Europe. In England however Julian would have been more familiar with devotion to the five wounds of Jesus which, as Richard Rolle's writings clearly show, contained a note of joy, notwithstanding their intrinsic link with the passion of Christ. Richard Rolle was a near-contemporary of Julian, a wandering hermit who wrote lyrically of the sweetness of loving Jesus, though his work does not have Julian's theological clarity and depth. He died of the plague when Julian was still a young girl, so it is possible that at least some of his writings were known to her, such as the following prayer:

Then was your body like unto heaven,
for, Jesus, as heaven is full of stars
so was your body full of wounds.
But, Lord, your wounds are better than stars,
for stars shine only by night,
and your wounds are full of virtue both day and night.
All stars shine but little
and a single cloud may hide them all;
but one of your wounds, sweet Jesus, is enough
to do away with the clouds of the whole of sinful humanity.
I beseech you Jesus, that these wounds
may be my meditation night and day;
for in your wounds is medicine
for each desire of my soul.
Sweet Jesus, your body is like a book
written all in red ink,
so is your body all written with red wounds.

Julian, with her deep love of the passion from girlhood and her desire to enter into its mystery ever more fully, was able to write of the time before her Shewings:

I thought I had already experienced something of the passion of Christ; yet, by the grace of God, I desired still more. I wished I had really been there with Mary Magdalen and the others who loved him, in order to see with my own eyes the passion that our Lord suffered for me. This was so I might be able to suffer with him as was granted to those who were near to him and loved him. For this reason I wanted to have a bodily vision through which I could understand better the physical pains of our Lord and the compassion of our Lady and of all his true lovers alive at the time who saw his pains. I wanted to have been one of them and have suffered with them. Apart from this I never had any other desire for a vision or revelation from God until my soul would depart from the body (for I believed that I would be saved by the mercy of God). The reason for this prayer was that after the vision I might more truly understand the passion of Christ. *(2:1)*

Julian's desire was answered in a way far beyond her wildest imaginings. But it would be a mistake to think of her as one visited continually with ecstatic experiences. She herself makes it clear that after the few hours of her revelations as she lay near death, hers was henceforward the dark way of faith. In the long years ahead she trod the path of the ordinary Christian who has to work at his or her prayer no matter what darkness or dryness is encountered. Prayer is a gift we give God to please *him*, to thank *him*, not necessarily something that pleases *us* on the sensory level.

Julian spent years praying and pondering on the passion and all it revealed of the goodness, love and mercy of God. She knew well that what had been given her was not just for herself, it was a treasure held in trust to share with her fellow Christians.

> Everything I am saying about myself I mean to say about all my fellow Christians, for I was taught that this is what our Lord intends it for. Therefore I beg you all for God's sake, and I advise you for your own benefit, that you stop thinking about the poor wretch to whom the vision was shown. Rather, powerfully, wisely and humbly contemplate God himself, who in his courteous love and in his goodness wanted to show these things to all, so that all might be comforted. It is God's will that you accept it with the greatest joy and delight as if Jesus himself had shown it to you. *(8:6)*

In the following pages I have arranged some of Julian's writings in the format of a way of the cross, both as an introduction to her thought and as a means of renewing and revivifying a traditional prayer form.

Today the site of Julian's anchorhold has been rebuilt and is an oasis of silence and contemplation for all who visit the place in her memory. Around the church life goes on as in any big city, but in the quiet of St Julian's there is time and space to gaze with Julian at the cross and with her choose Jesus. If we do this then all she has to say can be ours.

At this time I wanted to look away from the cross but I dared not, because I knew quite well that while I gazed at the cross I was secure and safe.

Then a suggestion was put into my mind in an apparently kindly manner: 'Look up to heaven to his Father'. With the faith I had I saw clearly that there was nothing between the cross and heaven that could have harmed me. I had therefore either look up or refuse to do so. I answered inwardly with all the power of my soul saying: 'I cannot, for you are my heaven'. I said this because I did not want to look up. I would rather have remained in pain until judgement day than enter heaven in any other way than through him.

I knew very well that he who bound me so painfully would unbind me when he wished.

In this way I was taught to choose Jesus for my heaven, whom I saw only in pain at that time. I wanted no other heaven than Jesus, who will be my bliss when I get there.

It has always been a great comfort to me that by his grace I chose Jesus to be my heaven throughout all this time of his passion and sorrow. This has taught me that I should always do so; choosing only Jesus to be my heaven through thick and thin. *(19:1-3)*

* * *

PRAYER

> *God of your goodness give me yourself,*
> *for you are enough for me.*
> *I cannot ask anything less to be worthy of you.*
> *If I were to ask less*
> *I should always be in want.*
> *Only in you have I all. (5:4)*

First Station

Jesus is condemned to death

Pilate, wishing to satisfy the crowd, released Barabbas for
them; and after flogging Jesus, he handed him over to be
crucified. *(Mk 15:15)*

Jesus stands before Pilate
humiliated and exhausted,
bruised and powerless.
A brigand and murderer
has been preferred before him.
Yet Jesus has done nothing but good;
healing, consoling, compassionating the multitudes.
But he has also alienated the religious leaders
who see him as a threat,
and so he must die.
This gentleness and freedom of his
has aroused their hatred and fear.

How quickly then the people clamour for his death!
It is easy to follow those who are popular
when their star is in the ascendant;
and easy too to turn against them
when we discover they are now out of favour,
and we worry about our own reputation or our family
if we continue to offer support.

The world is full of fearful people
with a little power;
full too of powerless men and women
who have identified themselves with Jesus
and who are even now persecuted,
imprisoned, tortured,
or simply among 'the disappeared'
because they took a stand for freedom
and refused to compromise their integrity.

In these situations
it is easy to become angry, vengeful, bitter.

Jesus takes the suffering meted out to him so unjustly
silently and calmly.
He willingly accepts to be condemned
as part of the Father's plan for our redemption.
He identifies himself with the 'little ones'.
He is both servant and son,
ready to do the Father's will at whatever cost.

Like Julian,
may we remember always
that Jesus has truly become one of us
and experienced in his heart and flesh
the meaning of suffering and rejection.
And because he has borne everything
without any desire for revenge
we know that in God there is no anger,
only total love and complete forgiveness.

All Jesus asks from us
is gratitude and joy
in all he has accomplished on our behalf.

Outwardly, he stands fettered and condemned;
inwardly he is free,
giving himself for us with a surrendered heart.
No one takes his life,
he lays it down of his own free will
with us, for us, as one of us.

*　　*　　*

Our good Lord has taken upon himself all our blame and
therefore our Father may not and will not assign more blame
to us than to his own beloved Son, Jesus Christ.
Jesus is in all that shall be saved and all that shall be saved are
in Jesus. All this is the work of God's love, together with
obedience, meekness, patience and the virtues which are
part of this work. *(51:27,29)*

Consider the worthiness of the Most High and that he, the

most worthy of all, was most fully reduced to nothing and most utterly despised. Now the most important point that we have to consider in the passion is to think and to register in our mind that he who suffered is God, and then reflect on these other two points which are less important: one is what he suffered and the other is for whom he suffered.

Jesus brought to my mind something of the sublimity and nobility of the glorious Godhead, and at the same time the preciousness and tenderness of his blessed body which is united to it, also the loathing our nature experiences when it is confronted with pain. For just as he was the most tender and most pure of all people, so he was the one who suffered most deeply and most intensely. He suffered for the sins of everyone that shall be saved. And he saw and grieved for everyone's sorrow, desolation and anguish out of kindness and love.

As long as he was capable of suffering, he suffered for us and grieved for us. And as I by his grace contemplated all this, I saw that the love in him which he has for our souls is so strong that he chose to suffer deliberately, indeed with great desire, and he endured all the suffering gently and joyfully.

When a soul touched by grace looks at it like this, it shall truly see that the pains of Christ's passion surpass all other pains: that is, all pains which will be turned to everlasting and supreme joy by the power of Christ's passion. *(20:1-3)*

Anger and friendship are two opposites. We must admit that he who dispells and destroys our anger and makes us meek and humble, must himself always be loving, humble and gentle. This is the opposite of anger.

I saw very clearly that where our Lord appears there comes peace and there is no place for anger. I could not see any anger in God, neither short-lived nor long-lasting. For truly, as I see it, if God were angry even for a moment, we could have neither life, nor place, nor healing. As truly we have our being from the eternal power and wisdom of God and from his eternal goodness, just as truly we have our safekeeping in his eternal power, wisdom and goodness. Though we may feel in ourselves anger, disagreement and strife, yet we are all

enfolded in God's mildness and humility, in his kindness and graciousness.
I saw clearly that our everlasting friendship, our home, our life and our being are in God. The same everlasting goodness that keeps hold of us when we sin so that we do not perish, that same everlasting goodness continually gives us peace instead of all our anger and perverse feelings.   *(49:1-3)*

*   *   *

PRAYER
> *O Jesus,*
> *take from my heart*
> *all unforgivingness, anger and bitterness,*
> *all condemnation of others,*
> *all railing against life and what it brings.*
> *Fill me instead with joy*
> *when, like you, I have an opportunity*
> *to bear suffering,*
> *just as you rejoice now*
> *in the wondrous accomplishment*
> *of the work of salvation.*
> *You were condemned out of love for us,*
> *teach me patience*
> *by sharing your own patience with me.   Amen*

Second Station

SECOND STATION

Jesus accepts the Cross

Then the soldiers led Jesus into the courtyard of the palace
(that is, the governor's headquarters) and they called
together the whole cohort. And they clothed him in a purple
cloak; and after twisting some thorns into a crown, they put
it on him. And they began to salute him saying 'Hail, king of
the Jews!' They struck his head with a reed, spat upon him,
and knelt down in homage to him. After mocking him, they
stripped him of the purple cloak and put his own clothes on
him. Then they led him out to crucify him. *(Mk 15:16-20)*

Jesus is mocked and crowned as a king,
before he receives the cross
which will become his throne.
It is one thing to take up a cross
with grandeur
and to go forward with dignity.
It is quite other to be laughed at
and diminished by ridicule;
to know oneself the butt of jokes and buffoonery
while your heart breaks with bewilderment
and your body is bruised and bloody.

When I contemplate the thorn-crowned head
bowed under the weight of the cross
I can only marvel at the way
Jesus has become so approachable
because so needy.

It is my sins he bears
as he enfolds the cross.
For me he becomes helpless and weak.
And I?
I cannot accept the least misunderstanding,
the slightest rebuke.
I lose control and lash out at others
or I sink into fruitless despair.

I need to receive the seal of the cross,
to have it imprinted
deep within my heart.
Only love can enable me to be with Jesus.
Then I shall not only accept
the cross he has planned for me,
I shall embrace it with joy.

For the world has need of many
who do not rail against suffering
but who, with Jesus, take their share
and more than their share,
transmuting it into gentleness
and courteous self-offering,
refusing to repay injury with injury,
hurt with hurt.

This isn't possible
if we rely on our own strength.
It becomes possible through contemplating Jesus,
the thorn-crowned Jesus,
as Julian did:
in his surrender,
his humility,
and in his supreme 'friendliness'
towards us.

*　　*　　*

I saw with my bodily eyes the head of Christ continuously
and heavily bleeding. The great drops of blood fell down
from under the crown like pellets which looked as if they
came from the veins. When they came out they were of a
brownish-red colour (for the blood was very thick) and as
they spread they became bright red. Then when they reached
the eyebrows they vanished. Yet the bleeding continued
until I had seen and understood many things. Nevertheless,
the beautiful and life-like head continued in the same beauty
and vividness without any diminishment.

This vision was real and lifelike, horrifying and fearful, sweet and lovely. And what gave me most encouragement on the whole vision was the knowledge that our good Lord, who is so holy and awesome, is also so homely and courteous. And it is this that most filled my soul with delight and assurance. It seems to me that there can surely be no greater joy than that the one who is highest and mightiest, noblest and most worthy, should also be the one who is most lowly, humble, homely and courteous. And surely and truly he will make this marvellous joy our own when we shall see him. It is our good Lord's will for us that we believe and trust, enjoy and delight, comfort and solace ourselves as best we can (by the help of his grace) until the time that we see him in reality. (7:2,5,7)

God showed me that we have two kinds of sickness. One is impatience or sloth, because we let our burdens and sufferings weigh on us too much and too heavily. The other is despair or doubtful fear.
As a help against these, our Lord very humbly showed me the patience that he had in his cruel passion and also the joy and delight that he has in the passion because of love. He showed me this as an example of how we should gladly and wisely bear our pains, for that is very pleasing to him and very beneficial to us. The reason we are so burdened by these is because we are ignorant of love.
This happens because we remain looking at ourselves and at the sins we have committed in the past, sins which may have been deadly. Then because we do not keep our promises, or are unable to keep the purity in which our Lord has placed us, but often fall back into great wretchedness, we feel too ashamed to mention it. The thought of all this makes us so sorry and depressed that we can hardly find any comfort.
Sometimes we take this fear for humility, but it is a shameful blindness and weakness. We do not know how to despise it as we do any other sin which we recognise. This comes through lack of true judgement and is contrary to the truth. For of all the attributes of the Blessed Trinity, it is God's will that we have most confidence and delight in love.
For love makes power and wisdom very meek to us. For just

as God in his courtesy forgets our sin after we have repented, so likewise he wishes us to forget our sin, especially as far as our unreasonable depression and doubtful fears are concerned. *(73:2,3,5-7)*

*   *   *

PRAYER
Jesus,
teach me to look always at you.
May your thorncrowned head
remind me continually of your outpoured love,
your courtesy and humility.
May I accept patiently
the sufferings that are part of my own life,
knowing that I do so
in union with you
who have carried the cross before me.
When I am weighed down by doubts,
or laziness or depression,
may I find comfort
in the knowledge that I am forgiven.
Then I will be able to forgive myself
and find renewed peace and joy.   Amen

Third Station

Jesus falls the first time

Surely he has borne our infirmities
and carried our diseases;
yet we accounted him stricken,
struck down by God and afflicted.
But he was wounded for our transgressions,
crushed for our iniquities;
upon him was the punishment that made us whole,
and by his bruises we are healed.   *(Is.53:4,5)*

The falls of Jesus
are not mentioned in the gospels,
but commemorating them is a way of saying
that, humanly speaking,
he really experienced weakness.
It wasn't just a matter of shouldering the cross
and marching off to Calvary
like some superman.
And anyone, after such brutal treatment
would stumble and fall many times
under a heavy weight.

Maybe we expect too much of ourselves
and others
when we impatiently look for and demand
instant perfection, instant success.
Everything takes time.
There will always be setbacks;
occasions when we feel helpless
or useless or unable to cope.

We cannot conquer our sinfulness and addictions
just by making up our minds to be better.
There is no speedy formula available.
We have to taste and savour our weakness,
to cry out for grace and mercy
rather than relying on our own will power;

and grace is always pure gift,
given as and when God wants.

Whether we are feeling successful
or a failure,
God's supporting hand is there.
He knows we are human and fallible
because he made us that way.
Falling isn't so important,
what matters is getting up and going on
even when, like Jesus,
we are dirty and exhausted,
looking and feeling foolish.

Nobody minds suffering like a hero
but that's not how Jesus suffered.
He suffered as one who was truly
without any resources of his own,
who had to rely utterly
on grace given by the Father,
from moment to moment.

Julian sees clearly
that in our mortal life
there will always be 'ups and downs'.
But no matter what transpires
we can be sure we are kept safe
by the One who loves us unconditionally
—and forever.

*　　*　　*

God infused into my soul a most wonderful spiritual delight.
I was completely filled with an awareness of everlasting
security in which I was sustained without any painful fear.
This feeling was so glad and so spiritual that I was totally at
peace, at ease and at rest, so that there was nothing on earth
that could have grieved me.
This state lasted only for a short while, then all changed.
I was left all alone, deeply depressed and tired of my life,

so weary of myself that I could hardly bear to go on living. There was no comfort or calm for me now, only faith, hope and love: and these I did not feel, I only believed they were true.

Then soon after this our blessed Lord once again gave me comfort and rest for my soul. This was so satisfying and certain, so blissfully happy and powerful that no fear, no sorrow, no physical or spiritual pain of any kind could upset me. Then again I felt the pain, and then again delight and joy. Now one, now the other, repeatedly, I suppose about twenty times. In the times of joy I could have said with St Paul: 'Nothing shall separate me from the love of Christ', and in the pain I could have said with St Peter: 'Lord save me, I am perishing'.

I understood that this vision was shown to teach me that it is good for some souls to feel like this, up in the air then down in the dumps; sometimes strengthened, sometimes desolate and abandoned. God wants us to know that he keeps us always safe in bad and good times alike. And for the good of our souls we are sometimes left to ourselves, even though our sin may not always be the cause of it.   *(15:1-4)*

I thought to myself 'If there had been no sin, we should all have been pure and clean like our Lord, as he created us'. And so, in my foolishness, before this time I had often wondered why God, with his great foresight and wisdom, did not prevent the beginning of sin in the first place. For then, I thought, all would have been well.

This curious wondering would have been better left alone, but instead I mourned and grieved over it without reason or discretion. But Jesus, who in this vision instructed me in all that I needed to know, answered me with this word and said: 'Sin is necessary, but all shall be well and all shall be well, and all manner of things shall be well'.

By this bare word 'sin' our Lord meant me to understand in general all that is not good. It includes the shameful contempt and the uttermost tribulation that our Lord endured for us in this life, his death with all his pains and the suffering of all his creatures both in spirit and in body. For all of us are at times distressed and we shall continue to be so

27

(like Jesus our master) until we are wholly purified in our mortal flesh and in all our interior affections that are not wholly good. *(27:1,3)*

It is absolutely necessary for us to see that left to ourselves we are nothing at all but sin and wretchedness. And so, in seeing the lesser part of the sin which the Lord shows us, the greater part, which we do not see, is eliminated. For in his courtesy he sets a limit to what he allows us to see, because sin is so vile and horrible that we could not endure to see it as it is. So by this humbling knowledge, through contrition and grace, we shall be torn away from all that is not our Lord. Then our blessed Saviour will completely heal us and make us one with him.

This breaking and healing our Lord intends for all humankind. For the one who is highest and closest to God can see themselves with me as sinful and needy. And I, who am the least and lowest of those to be saved, can be comforted along with the one who is highest. So our Lord unites us in love. *(78:4,5)*

*　　*　　*

PRAYER

> *Jesus,*
> *you have experienced*
> *weakness and pain.*
> *You who are the sinless one*
> *have borne our infirmities*
> *and carried our sorrows.*
> *I cannot understand the mystery of suffering*
> *but I believe you are present in everything,*
> *and have undergone your passion*
> *out of love for us.*
> *Teach me to persevere in following you,*
> *confident that in some mysterious way,*
> *even though sin is the root and cause*
> *of all pain,*
> *all shall be well*
> *and all manner of things shall be well. Amen.*

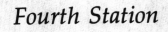

Fourth Station

Jesus meets his Blessed Mother

Is it nothing to you, all who pass by?
Look and see
if there is any sorrow like my sorrow?
For these things I weep;
my eyes flow with tears:
for a comforter is far from me,
one to revive my courage.
My children are desolate
for the enemy has prevailed.   *(Lam.1:12,16)*

Have we even the faintest idea
what it must have been like for Jesus and Mary
to share this bittersweet meeting
on the road to Calvary?

Most of us can bear some pain ourselves
if we have to do so,
but it is far worse
to see those we love suffering.

Jesus was flesh of Mary's flesh.
She loved him with a tenderness and selflessness
that must have made it well-nigh unbearable for her
to see him bowed under the weight of the cross.
And he who was so sensitive and compassionate
towards the widow of Naim
must have had his own agony increased
when he saw the agony of this widow
who was his own mother.

It is a diabolical thing
when people torture the spouse and children
of their victim
in order to break the spirit
of the one they want to subdue.
It is painful beyond words for a mother
who can only sit beside her dying child

and wait for the last breath
to depart from the innocent body.
So how can we plumb the anguish
felt by this mother and this son?

But Mary lets Jesus go.
She has to let him be about his Father's business,
as he has been all his conscious life.
She cannot, will not
do anything to hinder him.
She will keep and ponder this meeting in her heart
until the day of Resurrection.

There is so much we do not understand;
we can only support our loved ones mutely
and be there for them.

Julian sees Mary as all God's
from her first 'Fiat' at the Annunciation
to Calvary,
and to glory.
Mary shares everything with Jesus;
she wants only the Father's will as he does,
and this is why she is our model.
In Mary we see how we are loved
and summoned to share in the mystery of redemption.

*   *   *

He brought our lady St Mary to my attention. I saw her
spiritually in bodily likeness, a simple humble maiden, young
in years and little more than a child, in the form in which she
was when she conceived. God also showed me something of
the wisdom and truth of her soul, and through this I understood her sense of reverence with which she beheld God, her
creator. I also understood her profound wondering reverence
that he, her creator, should want to be born of her, someone
so simple and of his own making. This wisdom and truth, this
knowledge of her creator's greatness and her own littleness
as creature made her say to Gabriel in deep humility: 'Behold

32

me here, God's handmaiden!'. In this vision I understood without any doubt that, as far as worthiness and wholeness are concerned, she is superior to everything else God has made. For above her in the created order there is nothing except Jesus Christ in his humanity, as I see it. *(4:4)*

I saw something of the compassion of our lady St Mary, for Christ and she were so one in love that the greatness of her love was the cause of the greatness of her pain. In this I saw the substance of natural love developed by grace, which his creatures have for him. This natural love was most supremely and surpassingly shown in his sweet mother. For as much as she loved him more than others her pain surpassed all others. For always the higher, the stronger, the sweeter love is, the greater is the sorrow of one who sees the body of a beloved suffer. So all his disciples and true lovers suffered far more when he suffered than when they themselves died. I am sure, from the way I feel myself, that the very least of them loved him so much more than they loved themselves that I am unable to put it into words. *(18:1)*

Our good Lord looked down to his right side and brought to my mind where our Lady stood at the time of his passion and he said 'Would you like to see her?' and this sweet word sounded as if he said 'I know quite well that you would like to see my blessed mother, because after myself she is the highest joy I could show you. She is the greatest pleasure and honour to me, and the one whom all my blessed creatures most desire to see'. And because of the unique, exalted and wonderful love that he has for this sweet maiden, his blessed mother our Lady St Mary, he showed her bliss and joy through this sweet word, as if he said 'Would you like to see how I love her, so that you can rejoice with me in the love I have for her and she for me?'
And also to understand this sweet word better, our good Lord speaks to all people who shall be saved as if they were one single person. By this he seemed to say: 'Do you want to see in her how much you are loved? It is for love of you that I have created her so exalted, so noble, so worthy. This pleases me and I wish that you too be pleased with it'. For after

33

himself she is the most blissful sight. But here I was not taught that I should long to see her physical presence whilst I am on earth, but rather to see the virtues of her blessed soul; her truth, her wisdom, her love, through which I will know myself and reverently fear God. *(25:1,2)*

So our Lady is our mother, and in Christ we are all enclosed in her and born of her; because she who is the mother of our Saviour is the mother of all who are being saved by our Saviour. And our Saviour is our true mother, in whom we are continually being born and we shall never come out of him. *(57:5)*

*   *   *

PRAYER
> *Praise to you, true body sprung*
> *From the virgin Mary's womb;*
> *The same that on the cross was hung*
> *Bearing for us bitter doom.*
> *O most kind, most loving One,*
> *Sweetest Jesu, Mary's Son.*

> *You whose side was pierced and flowed*
> *Both with water and with blood,*
> *Suffer us of you to taste*
> *When we lie in death's embrace.*
> *O most kind, most loving One,*
> *Sweetest Jesu, Mary's Son.*   (Ancient prayer)

Fifth Station

Simon of Cyrene helps Jesus carry the Cross

They compelled a passer-by, who was coming in from the fields, to carry his cross; it was Simon the Cyrenian, the father of Alexander and Rufus.   *(Mk.15:21)*

Bear one another's burdens, and in this way you will fulfil the law of Christ.   *(Gal.6:2)*

Simon wasn't on the look out
to help anyone.
He just happened to be coming along.
Maybe he was in Jerusalem for Passover
for the first time.
Maybe it was a special event
planned for, saved for, longed for.
And now his great religious moment was spoiled.
He was seized on to help a criminal
carry a cross to execution.

And yet
Simon must have looked back later
and realised that this was the best,
not the worst moment of his life.
It seems that he became a believer
and his sons were known to the Christian community.

Sometimes we too can feel
that our great religious moments
are spoiled by human failings,
by some chance happening,
by our routine being upset.
People impinge on us
and we want them out of the way
so that we can proceed
with our own plans and projects.

If only we could accept everyone
as being sent to us by God

we would not be so selfishly intent
on finding him where he isn't.
Instead we would discover him in the needy,
the suffering,
those who get in our way
and thwart our designs.

We acknowledge that we also have burdens;
and how our hearts are gladdened
when someone, friend or stranger,
offers to lend a hand without being asked.
We know how grateful we are
when others put up with
or overlook our faults,
faults such as finnickiness, bad temper, touchiness.
We appreciate the care that is given
when we are in pain,
when we are anxious or depressed.
Why then can we not do the same for others?

Julian sees each one of us
as burdened by many failings.
These are part of what it means to be human.
Perhaps we have faults of character
that can't be remedied,
disabilities of one kind or another,
wounds left from childhood traumas.

These are not sins but humiliating weaknesses:
they are our share of the cross of Christ.
Jesus knows what it is to be weighed down
and to need help carrying a heavy burden.
If we offer compassion to one another
when the opportunity arises
we offer compassion to Christ;
just as, when others compassionate us
we receive from them
the tenderness of Jesus himself
who is living within them.

*   *   *

I saw how Christ has compassion on us because of our sins. And just as before I was full of pain and compassion because of the passion of Christ, so now I was full of compassion for my fellow Christians.

Yes, I saw clearly that our Lord even rejoices with pity and compassion over the tribulations of his servants. And on each person he loves and wants to bring to bliss, he lays something that in his eyes is not a defect yet makes them to be humiliated, despised, scorned, mocked and rejected in this world. And this he does to prevent them being harmed by the pomp, the pride and the vainglory of this wretched life, and to better prepare them for the way that will bring them to heaven with infinite joy and eternal bliss. For he says 'I shall completely break you of your empty affections and from your vicious pride and then I shall gather you to myself and make you humble and gentle, pure and holy, through oneing you to me.

And then I saw that every natural compassion anyone has for a fellow Christian is due to Christ living within; and every bit of the self-emptying that he revealed in his passion was shown again in this compassion. In this there were two different kinds of understanding in our Lord's meaning: one is the bliss to which we shall be brought and in this he wants us to rejoice, the other is the comfort in our pain. For he wants us to know that it shall all be transformed for us into glory and profit by the power of his passion, and to know that we do not suffer alone but with him. *(28:1-3)*

The soul that wants to remain peaceful when other people's sins come to mind should drive them away as if they were the pains of hell and seek God's help against these thoughts. Reflecting on other people's sins creates a sort of thick fog in front of the eyes of the soul. As long as this lasts we are unable to see God's beauty unless we look at these sins with the sinner's deep repentance.

Whether we are filthy or clean, we are always the same in his love. Whether for good or for bad he never wants us to run away from him. *(76:2,4)*

At that time I was shown by God all our frailty and our falling, our betrayals and our denials, our scorn and our burdens, and all the misery that I thought could possibly happen in this life. Along with this he showed his blessed power, his blessed wisdom and the blessed love with which he watches over us in these difficult times; with the same tenderness and sweetness, for his own honour and with the same security for our salvation, as he raises us spiritually to the heights of heaven, turning everything to his glory and to our joy forever. *(62:1)*

If I look at myself I am nothing at all, but in the whole body of Christ I am, I hope, united in love with all my fellow-Christians. It is on this union of love that the life of all those who are going to be saved depends. *(9:1)*

*   *   *

PRAYER
>*Jesus,*
>*I find it so easy to pass judgement on others,*
>*so difficult to come forward*
>*and offer help and forgiveness.*
>*Give me a living faith in your presence*
>*abiding in each person I encounter.*
>*May I see with your eyes,*
>*understand with your mind,*
>*love with your heart*
>*all who touch my life;*
>*and may we bear one another's burdens*
>*with patience. Amen*

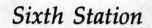

Sixth Station

SIXTH STATION

Veronica wipes the face of Jesus

I gave my back to those who struck me,
and my cheeks to those who pulled out the beard;
I did not hide my face
from insult and spittle.   *(Is.50:6)*

Legend recounts
that on the way to Calvary
a woman came forward,
braving mockery and contempt,
and wiped the face of Jesus,
(bruised and tortured as it was)
with a piece of cloth.
Afterwards she discovered
a likeness of that suffering face
imprinted on the linen.
Hence the woman was given the name of Veronica
which means 'true image' (vera icon).

It is not difficult to find in this lovely legend
a core truth of Christ's teaching:
that what we do for others
is done for him.
So acts of kindness and mercy
gradually form us
into the likeness of Jesus himself,
even though we do not realise it at the time.

But Julian sees another significance
in Veronica's veil.
Beneath his suffering humanity
Jesus was hidden from us as God.
He put aside his radiant glory
to become as we are.
That is why we often miss his presence,
do not recognise him
in what is unlovely, ugly, disfigured.

While we are on earth
the face of Jesus is not seen clearly
in its true beauty.
It is disguised,
not immediately obvious,
and so we are driven to seek him in faith
beneath changing outward appearances.

If we, like Veronica,
are always at the ready
to do a kindness,
we will discover
that Jesus leaves his imprint upon us
in the most unlikely situations and encounters.
Seeking him like this
is as good as seeing him in the flesh.

Jesus is present in all our searching
and under many disguises.
If we believe this
we cannot help but seek
with gladness and confidence,
knowing that one day this face of sorrow
will be turned towards us
in joy and gratitude.

*   *   *

I saw with bodily sight, in the face of the crucifix that hung
before me and at which I continually gazed, part of Christ's
passion. I saw there insults, spittle and dirt, bruises and
many long drawn out pains more than I can tell, and frequent
changes of colour in the face. Then I saw how half of the face,
beginning at the ear, was covered with dried blood which
formed a kind of crust as far as the middle of the face. After
that the other half was covered in the same way. Then it
vanished in the first part just as it had come.
It made me think of the holy veil of Veronica in Rome on
which he imprinted his own blessed face when, during his
passion, he was voluntarily going to his death, often changing

in colour from brown to black, his face sorrowful and wasted. Seeing this veil many people were amazed and asked themselves how it were possible that this could be the image of his blessed face which is the most beautiful in heaven, the flower of earth and the fruit of the virgin's womb. How could this image then be so discoloured and so far from beautiful? I wish to tell you what I, by the grace of God, understood it to mean. We know from our faith and from the preaching and teaching of holy church that the Blessed Trinity made humankind in its own image and likeness. Similarly we know that when we fell so deeply and so wretchedly through sin, there was no help to restore us save through the One who created us. And the One who created us for love, by the same love wanted to restore us to the same blessedness and even more. And just as we were made like the Trinity in our first making, so our Creator wanted us to be like our Saviour Jesus Christ in heaven and live there forever by the power of our recreation. Then between these two creations he wanted, out of love and respect for us, to make himself as much like us in this mortal life with all its wretchedness and filth as could be possible without sin. It was the image and likeness of our death, foul and black, in which our blessed Lord, fair and radiant, hid his godhead. *(101:5,6)*

I see in our Lord's face three kinds of expression.
The first is the expression of the passion as he showed it when he was with us in this life at the time of death. And although this sight is mournful and sorrowful, yet it remains glad and joyful because he is God.
The second expression is pity, tenderness and compassion. This he shows to all his lovers with the assurance of complete protection for those who are in need of his mercy.
The third expression is that blessed face as it shall be without end. This was shown most often and continued for the longest period of time.
And so when we are in pain and distress he reveals to us the face of his passion and his cross, helping us to bear our own with his own blessed power. And when we sin he shows us the expression of pity and compassion, powerfully protecting and defending us against all our enemies. These are the two

usual expressions that he shows us in this life. Mixed with them is the third, namely that blessed face partially what it will be in heaven. This comes about by the touch of grace and the sweet enlightenment of the spiritual life, through which we are kept in true faith, hope and love, in contrition and in devotion, as well as in contemplation and in all the different kinds of true joy and sweet consolations. The blessed face of God our Lord does all this in us through his grace.   *(71:3-5)*

I saw him and I sought him. I had him and I lacked him. And this is and shall be our ordinary way of life as I see it.   *(10:2)*

*   *   *

PRAYER
> *Jesus*
> *teach me to recognise you everywhere*
> *and in everyone.*
> *May I live so closely in your company*
> *that others may recognise you*
> *in my own face,*
> *my own expression,*
> *just as those who live together*
> *over a long period of time*
> *take on one another's likeness.*
> *Let me not turn away from you*
> *no matter what disguise you come in.*
> *Imprint your image on my heart*
> *that I may become your true icon.   Amen*

Seventh Station

Jesus falls the second time

He drove into my heart
the arrows of his quiver;
I have become the laughingstock of all peoples,
the burden of their songs all day long.
He has filled me with bitterness,
he has sated me with wormwood.
He has made my teeth grind on gravel,
and made me cower in ashes;
my soul is bereft of peace,
I have forgotten what happiness is.   *(Lam.3:13-17)*

Falling and rising alternate
on the journey we travel through life.
Sometimes we seem
to be full of strength and courage,
ready to face anything;
at other times
we feel weak and powerless,
without resources, without hope.

Jesus too knew what it was like
to have to get up and keep going
when he must have been tempted
to simply sink down to the ground
and abandon the struggle.
He did not sin
but he has borne our sins
and experienced their weight.
Sin has prostrated him beneath the cross.

Often we take this truth for granted.
We have let the story of the passion
become too familiar.
We do not ponder on the reality of sin
and the price Jesus has paid.
Or if we do ponder on sin's reality
we get depressed,

feeling helpless and hopeless
in the face of our shabbiness.

Julian reminds us
that, though we sin,
we are ever held secure,
safe in the love of God.
His love does not depend on our 'being good'
much less on our 'being perfect'.
His is a love that is total,
unconditional,
unbreakable.
Through our sin we discover
the dependability of God's love.
We experience his forgiveness
in being restored to grace
and, in Julian's thought,
the wounds left by sin
become honourable scars,
just as the wounds of Jesus
shine now in his glorified body.

When we understand how securely and tenderly
we are held by the love of God
sin loses its attraction.
But there is a lesson to be learned
and a price to be paid.
The price is that, secure in God's acceptance
we too must forgive others their sins and failings
as we have been forgiven.
For the human race is bonded person to person,
and we fall and are redeemed
not just individually,
but together.

*   *   *

Even though our Lord showed me that I would sin, by 'me
alone' is meant all. And in this I felt a gentle fear rising in me
to which our Lord answered 'I keep you very safe'.

This word was spoken to me with love and a guarantee of spiritual protection greater than I can or may tell. For just as I first was shown that I would sin, so was I shown comfort, security and protection for all my fellow Christians. What could make me love my fellow Christians more than to see in God that he loves all who are going to be saved as if they were one soul. *(37:2)*

And God showed me that sin shall not be to our shame but to our honour, because just as there is rightly a corresponding pain for every sin, so likewise there is given to the same soul by love a blessing for every sin. Just as different sins are punished with different pains according to their seriousness, likewise they shall be rewarded with different joys in heaven. For there are victories gained over sin according to the degree in which they have been the cause of pain and sadness for the soul here on earth. For the soul that shall come to heaven is so precious to God and its place in heaven is so glorious, that the goodness of God will never allow the soul to die in sin. *(38:1)*

Our good Lord protects us most tenderly when it seems to us that we are almost forsaken and cast off because of our sins and because we see that we have deserved it. Yet because of the humility that we learn from this we are raised very high in God's sight by his grace. Furthermore, those whom our Lord chooses he invites through his grace with such great contrition, compassion and true longing for the will of God, that they are suddenly delivered from sin and pain and taken up to bliss, being made equal with the saints.
By contrition we are made clean, by compassion we are made ready and by true longing we are made worthy. These are the three means, as I see it, by which souls get to heaven; that is to say, those who on earth have been sinners and are destined to be saved.
For every sinful soul must be healed by these medicines. And even though the sinner is healed, his wounds are still seen by God—not as wounds but as signs of honour. *(39:2-4)*

As much as God is powerful and wise to save us, equally much is he willing to do so. For Christ himself is the ground of all the laws of Christians and he taught us to do good in return for evil. Here we can see that he himself is this love, and he does for us what he teaches us to do. He wishes us to be like him in wholehearted, never ending love towards ourselves and our fellow Christians. Just as little as his love for us is broken off because of sin, so little does he want our love for ourselves and for our fellow Christians to be broken off. But we must forever hate sin and forever love the soul as God loves it. Then we shall hate sin as God hates it and love the soul as God loves it. For the words God said to me 'I will keep you safe' are an endless comfort.   *(41:5)*

*   *   *

PRAYER
> *Jesus,*
> *you knew what it was to fall and rise*
> *on the way to Calvary.*
> *You bore our sins with meekness*
> *and compassion.*
> *Forgive us our sins*
> *as we forgive those who sin against us;*
> *and may we be ever confident*
> *that you keep us safe,*
> *held and enfolded in love.*
> *No matter how often we fall,*
> *with you may we rise up*
> *and continue our journey*
> *with confidence and joy.   Amen*

Eighth Station

EIGHTH STATION

Jesus consoles the women of Jerusalem

A great number of people followed him, and among them were women who were beating their breasts and wailing for him.
But Jesus turned to them and said, 'Daughters of Jerusalem, do not weep for me but weep for yourselves and for your children. For the days are surely coming when they will say "Blessed are the barren, and the wombs that never bore, and the breasts that never nursed". Then they will begin to say to the mountains, "Fall on us"; and to the hills "Cover us". For if they do this when the wood is green, what will happen when it is dry?'   *(Lk.23:27-31)*

These women may have been professional mourners
employed to accompany condemned criminals
with wailing and lamentation.
Or they may have been bystanders
moved to tears at the fate of a man
who had always treated women
as persons worthy of respect.

Whoever they are
they represent Jerusalem,
the city Jesus loves.
He has hoped and longed
to hold and gather her people
as a hen gathers her chicks under her wings,
or as a mother enfolds her children
in the skirts of her garment.
Yet this city of predilection
has condemned him,
and is casting him outside its walls
to die in ignominy and pain.

Jesus has already shed tears over Jerusalem.
These weeping women see only
his approaching death,
while he sees the grief that must be theirs

when the whole city is destroyed
and its people starved into surrender.
If Jesus, the innocent one,
suffers so cruelly,
what must be the fate of the guilty?
What will become of these women
and their innocent children?
His heart bleeds to think of it,
and so he forgets himself
in his anguish over them.
This is true selflessness.

Julian, like Jesus,
sees everything as being part
of the plan of a loving Father.
We too mourn and weep,
we sorrow for ourselves and others,
but the deepest reality is bliss.
God's providence is always at work,
hidden but sure.

Like the women of Jerusalem
we now see the face of Jesus
buffeted, torn, despised
as he looks upon us.
But one day, together,
we will see him in glory.
Then every tear will be wiped away
and there will be no more weeping
or crying or mourning
for the former things will have passed away.

*   *   *

Our Lord wants the soul to turn around and sincerely contemplate him in all his works. For they are totally good and all his decrees are easy and sweet. They bring great peace to those that have turned away from contemplating the blind pronouncements of mortals to focus on the delightful and lovely decrees of the Lord our God. We may see some deeds

as well done and others as evil, but our Lord does not see
them like this. For just as all that exists in nature is the work
of God, so all deeds bear the stamp of God's doing. It is easy
to understand that the best of deeds is well done; but the
most insignificant deed that is being done is done just as well
as the best and the greatest. Everything is according to the
quality and the order ordained by God even before the world
began. For there is no doer but God.
I saw with absolute certainty that he never changes his
purpose in anything, nor ever will without end. For there
was nothing unknown to him in his rightful ordering of
things from the very beginning. Therefore everything was set
in order before anything was made, so that it would endure
forever. And no manner of thing will fall short on this
principle, because he has made all things perfectly good.
And therefore the blessed Trinity is always fully pleased with
all its works. God revealed all this to me with great happiness
as if to say: 'See, I am God. See, I am in all things. See, I do
all things. See, I never lift my hands from my works nor ever
shall without end.'   *(11:3-6)*

Even though our Lord God dwells now in us and is here with
us, though he calls us and enfolds us in his tender love so
that he can never leave us, though he is nearer to us than
tongue can tell or heart can thirst, yet we shall never cease
mourning and weeping, nor seeking nor longing, until we
can clearly look at him in his blessed face. In that precious
sight there can be no more grief nor any lack of wellbeing.
In this I saw cause for both laughter and tears. Cause for
laughter because our Lord and Creator is so near to us (and is
in us) and we are in him through the fidelity with which he
watches over us in his goodness.
Cause for tears because our spiritual eye is so blind and we
are so weighed down with heaviness in our mortal flesh and
in the darkness of sin that we cannot clearly see the blessed
face of our Lord God. No, and because of this darkness we
can hardly believe or trust in his great love nor be sure of his
faithful protection of us. And it is for this reason that I say we
can never cease mourning and weeping.
This 'weeping' does not simply mean shedding physical tears

57

from our bodily eyes; it also has a more spiritual meaning. For the natural desire of the soul is so great and so immeasurable that, if we were given for our enjoyment and comfort all the finest things that God ever created in heaven or on earth, but could not see his lovely and blessed face, then we should nevertheless never cease to mourn and weep in the spirit out of painful longing until we finally and truly saw the beautiful and blessed face of our Maker. And if on the other hand we were in all the pain that heart can think or tongue can tell and at the same time could see his beautiful and blessed face, then none of the pain would upset us.
So that blessed sight is the end of every kind of pain for the loving soul, and the fulfilment of every kind of joy and bliss. (72:3-6)

*   *   *

PRAYER
> *Jesus,*
> *the women of Jerusalem*
> *mourned over you*
> *as you went to your death,*
> *but your concern was not for yourself*
> *but for them.*
> *You knew that all was part of the Father's plan,*
> *that all was 'well done'*
> *even when it involved pain.*
> *Help me to disregard my own sufferings*
> *so as to reach out to others;*
> *and may I discern your presence*
> *in all that happens*
> *here on earth.   Amen*

Ninth Station

Jesus falls the third time

It is good that one should wait patiently
for the salvation of the Lord.
It is good for one to bear the yoke in youth,
to sit alone in silence
when the Lord has imposed it,
to put one's mouth in the dust
(there may yet be hope),
to give one's cheek to the smiter
and be filled with insults.
For the Lord will not reject forever.
Although he causes grief, he will have compassion
according to the abundance of his steadfast love;
for he does not willingly afflict or grieve anyone.

(Lam.3:26-33)

We could understand
one or even two falls.
But three? even more than three?
Surely that is pressing the point too much!
Here is real weakness, real prostration
even though help has been given by Simon of Cyrene.

But isn't this just like life?
we sin, we fall,
we determine not to sin again,
not to be overcome by weakness,
but we do,
we are—
twice, three times . . .
numberless times.
How frail we are!
How fragile our good resolutions!

Jesus is with us even here.
He too has had his face in the dust,
been mocked, jeered at,
because he lacked the strength to succeed.
He goes to the cross experiencing failure

to the roots of his being.

We ourselves are so unstable, Julian says,
easily overpowered in temptation, sorrow, affliction.
We are so conscious of ourselves
and of our numerous failings
that God seems blotted out of the horizon.
But it is good to know,
deep in our flesh and spirit,
how much we are in need of help and strength.
We cannot save ourselves,
and so we experience our need for a Saviour.

Jesus has revealed to us
the gracious and merciful Father,
who never abandons us
no matter what we may have done.
And Jesus himself knows
what it is to be frail and weak,
to depend on grace and mercy
to finish the journey.

In him we are enabled
to get up and go on
even though, of ourselves,
we can't take another step.

*   *   *

In this life we are changeable, and because of our frailty, simplicity and foolishness we fall into sin. We are weak and unwise in ourselves. Also our will is overpowered when we find ourselves in temptation, sorrow and affliction. The cause of all this is blindness, because we do not see God. If we constantly saw God we would have no bad feelings, nor any kind of impulse or affliction that serves as an occasion for sin. (47:2)

Mercy, out of love, allows us to fall to a certain extent. And to the extent that we fail we fall, and to the extent that we fall we die. We must necessarily die inasmuch as we fail to see and feel God, who is our life. Our failing is dreadful, our falling is shameful, and our dying is sorrowful. Yet in all this the sweet eye of pity and love never turns away from us, and the work of mercy never fails. *(48:3)*

During our lifetime here on earth we have in us a marvellous mixture of good and bad. We have in us our Lord Jesus Christ and we have in us also the wretchedness and the harm of Adam's falling. In our dying we are all the time very securely upheld by Christ, and through his gracious touching we are raised to real trust in salvation. Because of Adam's fall our sensitivity is broken up in many different ways through sin and various pains, and this casts us into such darkness and blindness that we can hardly find any comfort. But we intend to stay with God and faithfully trust that he will give mercy and grace to us. This itself is God's working in us. In his goodness he opens for us the eye of understanding so that we can see sometimes more, sometimes less, according to the ability he gives us to receive it. Now we are raised into the one, and again we are allowed to fall into the other.

As a result of this extraordinary diversity of sentiments the mixture in us is so bewildering that we hardly know where we ourselves and our fellow Christians stand, except that we still say yes to God when we do sense him, truly willing to be with him with all our heart, with all our soul and with all our strength. Then we hate and despise our evil inclinations and all that may be an occasion of sin for us spiritually or physically. But even so, when this sweetness is hidden, we fall again into blindness and then into all kinds of sorrow and distress. However, this remains our comfort, for we know in our faith that through the power of Christ we never fully submit to this darkness, but we struggle against it, enduring in pain and sorrow, praying until the time that he shows himself again to us. And so we remain in this muddle all the days of our life. But he wants us to trust that he is always with us. *(52:2,3)*

We ought humbly to recognise our weakness, admit that we cannot stand on our own feet even for the twinkling of an eye without the help of grace, and reverently cling to God, trusting only in him.

For God sees one way and we see another way. It belongs to us humbly to accuse ourselves, while it belongs to the goodness of God graciously to excuse us. *(52:8,9)*

When we have fallen through frailty or blindness, then our courteous Lord raises us up with his gentle touch and protects us. He wants us to see how wretched we are and humbly face up to it. But he does not want us to stay like that, or to be preoccupied with self accusation or to wallow in self pity. For he wants us quickly to attend to him, for he stands all alone, and he is always waiting for us, sorrowing and grieving until we come. He hurries to bring us back to himself for we are his joy and his delight and he is our salvation and our life. *(79:5)*

*   *   *

PRAYER

> *Jesus,*
> *I fall so many times.*
> *Let me never cease believing in your grace and mercy,*
> *always ready to welcome me back*
> *and embrace me once more.*
> *Give me courage,*
> *rekindle my hope.*
> *Be my companion on life's journey*
> *as you want me to be yours.   Amen*

Tenth Station

Jesus is stripped of his garments

They took his clothes and divided them into four parts, one
for each soldier. They also took his tunic; now the tunic was
seamless, woven in one piece from the top. So they said to
one another, 'Let us not tear it, but cast lots for it to see who
will get it'. This was to fulfil what the scripture says,
'They divided my clothes among themselves,
and for my clothing they cast lots.'   *(Jn.19:23,24)*

Totalitarian regimes know what they are doing
when they strip their victims
before interrogation and torture.
To be without clothes is to be visibly vulnerable.
It takes away one's personal dignity
and sense of individual worth.
It makes one want to hide
before those who expose others.
One feels shamed and degraded
before the hard, unrelenting stares of interrogators,
the mocking laughs of tormentors.
Yes, nakedness can be terrible.

But there is another way of being naked,
the way of lovers.
Lovers want to be seen just as they are,
to be close to one another flesh to flesh.
That's hard to believe when it comes to God
and our relationship with him.
We busily dress ourselves up,
disguise our real selves,
trying to hide our nakedness from him,
like Adam and Eve in the garden of Eden.
We do not easily grasp that his gaze
is not the hard stare of the judge
but the tender embrace of the lover.

God wants us to cling to him so closely
that nothing can come between us.

Thus we realise
that all the artifices we use
to deck ourselves out,
hoping to catch his attention,
are totally useless.
Only God's self can satisfy us,
a God who embraces our nakedness and nothingness
and clothes us with his own goodness.

At this station
we see Jesus stripped and humbled before hostile eyes.
But Jesus' dignity is not dependent on clothing.
His garments are shared among the soldiers,
but the tender hands of the Father
weave around him a more glorious garment
that will be revealed at the right time.

Julian sees how Jesus has made himself humble
and ready to serve us.
He is like a mother
who swaddles her child
with her own hands,
attending to all her child's bodily needs
with tender care.
We are so preciously loved
that we have nothing to fear before our God,
who has been stripped and humbled before others
in order that we might realise
how precious we are in his sight.

*   *   *

At the same time as I had the bodily vision of the bleeding
head, our good Lord also gave me a spiritual vision of his
homely loving. I saw that he is to us everything that is good
and comfortable for our help. He is our clothing which for
love enwraps us and enfolds us, embraces us and fully
shelters us. With his tender love he is so close to us that he
can never leave us. So I saw in this vision that he is everything that is good as far as I could understand.

We need to be aware of the littleness of created things in order to avoid being attached to them and so come to love and possess God who is uncreated.

For this is the reason why we are not fully at ease in heart and soul. We seek rest in insignificant things which can offer us no rest, and we do not know God who is all-powerful, totally wise and good. He alone is true rest. God wishes to be known by us and he delights when we rest in him, for all that is less than him is not enough for us. This is the reason why no soul can be at rest until it is emptied of all created things. When the soul voluntarily and for love lets go of all created things in order to possess him who is all, then it is able to receive spiritual rest.   (5:1,4,5)

To centre on the goodness of God is the highest form of prayer, and God's goodness comes to meet us at our most basic need. It gives life to our soul and makes it live and grow in grace and virtue. It is nearest to us by nature and the readiest to bring us grace; for it is the same grace that the soul seeks and ever will, until the day in which we truly know God who has completely enfolded us in himself.

A person goes upright, and the food eaten is preserved in the body as in a most beautiful purse. When it is necessary the purse opens and then it shuts again in full honesty. And that it is God who does this is shown there where he says that he comes down to the lowest part of our need. For he does not despise what he has made, nor does he disdain to serve us even in the simplest of our natural bodily functions; for he loves the one he has made in his own likeness.

For just as the body is clad in clothes, and the flesh in skin, and the bones in the flesh and the heart in the whole, so are we, body and soul, clad and enclosed in the goodness of God. Yes, and even more intimately because all these other things will wear out and vanish, but the goodness of God is always whole and close to us without compare.

Truly our lover desires our soul to cling to him with all its might and to cling evermore to his goodness. For, of all the things the heart could think of, this pleases God most and helps the soul to prayerfulness. Our soul is so preciously loved by him who is highest that it is far beyond the comprehension of creatures. That is to say that no created being can fully know how much, how sweetly and how tenderly our Creator loves us. And therefore we can, with his grace and his help, remain in spiritual contemplation, endlessly marvelling at the high, surpassing, immeasurable love which our Lord in his goodness has for us. So we may reverently ask from our Lord all that we want; for our natural will is to have God, and the good will of God is to have us.   (6:2,3)

*   *   *

PRAYER

Jesus,
you were stripped of everything
so that I should be clothed in grace.
Your goodness is all around me,
cherishing me, enfolding me.
May I be enabled to want
nothing except yourself.
May I be prepared to let everything else
be stripped away
so that you alone may be
my God and my All.   Amen

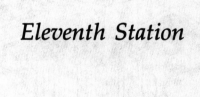

Eleventh Station

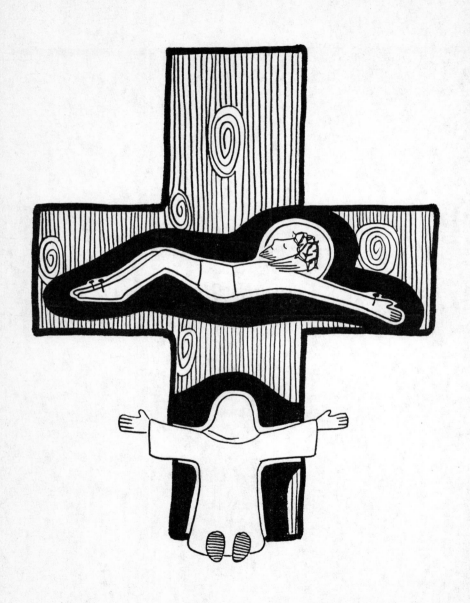

ELEVENTH STATION

Jesus is nailed to the Cross

Then they brought Jesus to the place called Golgotha (which means the place of the skull). And they offered him wine mixed with myrrh; but he did not take it.
It was nine o'clock in the morning when they crucified him. The inscription of the charge against him read, 'The King of the Jews'. And with him they crucified two bandits, one on his right and one on his left.   *(Mk.15:22,23,24-27)*
And Jesus said 'Father, forgive them; for they know not what they do'.   *(Lk.23:34)*

To be nailed to a cross is no joke.
Can we imagine the spasms of intense pain,
the gasps of agony,
the blood seeping through the torn flesh
as the nails are driven home and the cross raised?
Jesus has refused the drugged wine
so he feels the pain fully and consciously.

And yet he forgives his tormentors.
They did not know who he really was,
neither did they know the love
that had driven him to the cross.

In the book of Genesis we read
that the blood of Abel cried out from the ground,
calling for vengeance on Cain, his murderer.
But the blood of Jesus is poured out willingly
for the salvation of the world.
He has transmuted his torture into calm surrender
by offering his torturers
unconditional love and forgiveness.

The world is a Calvary where, even today,
Christ is nailed to a thousand crosses
between two bandits.
He is nailed in the Jewish mother,
forced into the gas chamber

with her child in her arms.
He is with the Arab, dispossessed and frustrated,
unable to provide for wife and children.
He is with the political prisoner
tortured in a nameless jail
by nameless tormentors.
He is with those persecuted for race, colour or religion,
gender or sexual orientation.

Jesus is nailed in those confined, immovable,
to a hospital bed,
dying from cancer or AIDS.
He is present in the helplessness and terror
of the abused child,
and he is present in the abuser,
who is held in the grip
of unconquerable needs and obsessions.

And for myself,
I feel the wounds of my past,
the sins I have committed
and the sins committed against me.
Can I forgive myself? Forgive others?
I am nailed to the cross of my own life
whether I wish it or not.
I want people to pity me,
instead of allowing myself
to accept the sufferings
that are, and have been mine.

I ask now for the grace
to open my hands without rebellion or resentment
as, with Julian,
I ponder on the precious blood
poured out for this world of pain.

*   *   *

The idea came to me that, out of the tender love God has for
us, he has created a vast supply of water on the earth for our
use and for our bodily comfort. Yet he much prefers that we

74

take for our perfect cure his blessed blood to wash ourselves clean from sin; for there has been no other liquid made which he would prefer to give us. It is most plentiful as it is most precious, and that by virtue of his blessed Godhead. It is of our own nature and blessedly flows over us by the power of his precious love.

The dearworthy blood of our Lord Jesus Christ is truly as plentiful as it is most precious. Behold and see the power of this precious abundance of his dearworthy blood. It descended down into hell, burst hell's chains and freed all who were there who belonged to the court of heaven. The precious abundance of his dearworthy blood flows over the whole world, ready to wash away all sin from every human being who is of good will, who has been and who will be. The precious abundance of his dearworthy blood rises up to heaven in the blessed body of our Lord Jesus Christ, and there it is now within him, bleeding and praying for us to the Father. *(12:2,3)*

Let us humbly cry out to our dear mother and he will sprinkle us all with his precious blood. He will make our soul most tender and gentle. And in the course of time he will most gently restore us to full health. This will bring great glory to him and endless joy to us. He will never leave or neglect doing this sweet work of love until all his beloved children are born and delivered. This was revealed when he taught me about the spiritual thirst, which is the love longing that will last until the Day of Judgement.

So our life is grounded in Jesus our true mother, in his own foreseeing wisdom from without beginning, together with the almighty power of the Holy Spirit. By taking our nature he gave us life, and in the blessed dying on the cross he brought us forth to eternal life.

Ever since then, now and always until Judgement Day, he feeds us and helps us, just as the high sovereign nature of motherhood demands and as the maternal need of childhood requires. Fair and sweet is our heavenly Mother in the eyes of our soul, precious and loving are the grace-filled children in the eyes of the homely Mother, with the gentleness and meekness and all the lovely virtues which belong to children by nature. For naturally the child does not despair of its mother's love and naturally the child does not rely on itself, and naturally the child loves its mother as the mother loves her child.

These are the beautiful virtues which, with all the others that are like them, serve and please our heavenly Mother. I saw that in this life there is no state greater in weakness and in lack of power and intelligence than the one of childhood, until the day when our Mother of grace brings us into the Father's bliss. And there it shall be made known to us what he means by these sweet words 'All shall be well: and you shall see for yourself that all manner of things shall be well'. Then the bliss of our motherhood in Christ will begin anew in the joys of God our Father, and this new beginning shall continue being renewed without end.

So I understood that all his blessed children who have been born of him by nature shall be brought back to him by grace. (63:3-7)

*   *   *

PRAYER

> *Jesus,*
> *when I contemplate your blood*
> *shed for us in such agony*
> *I remember that these were the birthpangs*
> *of a mother,*
> *who later forgets the pain*
> *for joy that a child has been born*
> *into the world.*
> *I have suffered so little*
> *and with such meanness and reluctance.*
> *Give me, I pray,*
> *a new heart and a new spirit,*
> *that, in union with you,*
> *I may become a mother*
> *whose pain bears fruit,*
> *and is lifegiving for the world.   Amen*

Twelfth Station

TWELFTH STATION

Jesus dies on the Cross

When Jesus knew that all was now finished he said (in order to fulfil the scripture) 'I am thirsty'. A jar full of sour wine was standing there. So they put a sponge full of the wine on a branch of hyssop and held it to his mouth. When Jesus had received the wine he said 'It is finished'. Then he bowed his head and gave up his spirit.   *(Jn.19:28-30)*

When the centurion saw what had taken place, he praised God and said 'Certainly this man was innocent.' And when all the crowds who had gathered there for the spectacle saw what had taken place they returned home beating their breasts.   *(Lk.23:47,48)*

We are so used to crucifixes and crosses.
We see them in churches and homes,
we see them in graveyards and on tombstones,
we see them decorated and gilded,
suspended from delicate chains
and hung around necks.
So often they don't really make any impact.

Julian helps us to see the dying Christ
through new eyes.
It is as if she is watching him,
standing there with Mary and John.
inviting us to enter the mystery
of the death agony of the Son of God.

With her we can contemplate the tender body
so cruelly tormented by thirst,
gasping out a last breath.
It is a body still young in years
and therefore desirous of life
with every nerve and fibre.

In this last battle
Jesus is dying slowly, agonisingly,

79

cold within and without.
Above all there is the face
under the thorn crown,
pierced, gouged,
'without beauty or majesty';
Jesus' suffering is pure suffering
as he awaits the hour of release and glory.

If we can contemplate the crucifix
and feel for the first time
something of the tragedy and injustice
of innocent suffering,
we will understand anew
what love really means.
Not our love for God
but God's love for us,
when he sent his Son
to be the sacrifice
that takes our sins away.   *(cf 1 Jn.4:10)*

*   *   *

Christ showed me something of his passion near the time of his death. I saw his sweet face all dry and bloodless with the pallor of death and then later deadly pale, pining away.
At last when death came his face turned blue and finally brownish blue as the flesh became more profoundly dead. For his passion showed itself to me most vividly in his blessed face and especially in his lips. I saw these four colours in his dear face which I had seen before so fresh, ruddy, healthy and lovely. It was a painful change to see this deep dying. His nostrils shrivelled together and dried up before my eyes and his dear body turned black and brown. All changed from his naturally beautiful, fresh and lifelike colour into dry dying. For when our blessed Saviour died on the cross, there was a harsh, dry wind and it seemed bitterly cold.
When all the precious blood that could pass from it had been bled out of that sweet body it was revealed to me that there still remained a certain amount of moisture in his sweet flesh.

The loss of blood, the anguish inside his body and the searing wind and bitter cold outside, all met together in Christ's sweet body. And as the hours passed, these four things, two inside and two outside, dried up Christ's flesh. Though his pain was bitter and sharp it lasted a very long time and it painfully dried up all the fluids in Christ's flesh. In this way, before my eyes, I saw the sweet flesh wither, bit by bit, with terrible suffering. And as long as there remained any vital fluid in Christ's flesh he went on suffering.

It seemed to me that with all this long drawn out pining away he had been dying and dead for seven nights, always on the point of death, always suffering the throes of death. When I say that it seemed to me he had been dead for seven nights I mean only that his sweet body was so discoloured, so dry, so shrivelled, so deathly and so pitiful that he might have been dead for a week, though he went on dying. It seemed to me that the drying of Christ's flesh was the worst pain and the last of his passion. *(Ch.16)*

As I saw Jesus dying like this, his words 'I thirst' came to my mind. I saw in Christ a double thirst: a physical one and a spiritual one.

This word was given to me to show the physical thirst, which I understood was caused by the drying of bodily moisture. For the blessed flesh and bones were left exposed without blood or moisture. The blessed body dried out all alone for a long time with the twisting of the nails and the weight of the body. I understood that, because of the tenderness of the sweet hands and the sweet feet, and by the large size, cruelty and hardship of the nails, the wounds grew wider, while the body, which had been hanging for so long, sagged under its weight. I saw the crown of thorns caked with dried blood, piercing and pressing into the head, with the sweet hair and dry flesh stuck fast to the thorns and the thorns shrivelling in the flesh.

In the beginning, when the flesh was still fresh and bleeding, the constant pressure of the thorns made the wounds open wide. I could see that the sweet skin and tender flesh, the hair and the blood, were all raised and loosened from the forehead, having been gouged by the thorns. They were

81

hanging as if they would soon have fallen whilst the body still had natural moisture. How this was caused I did not see, but I understood that it was caused by the sharp thorns and the way in which the crown had been so violently and hurtfully pressed down upon his head relentlessly and without pity. This caused the sweet skin and the flesh to break all in pieces and the hair to pull from the bones. It was torn into shreds like a cloth and it sagged down as if it would soon have fallen because it was so heavy and so loose. This caused me great sorrow and fear for I thought I would rather die than have it fall.

It seemed to me that the pain I now felt passed way beyond mere physical death. I thought 'Is there any pain in hell like this pain?' And I was answered in my reason 'Hell is a different pain, for there is despair'. But of all the pains that lead to salvation the greatest pain of all is to see the one you love suffer. How could there be any greater pain than to see him who is all my life, all my bliss, all my joy, suffer? I felt absolutely sure that I loved Christ more than myself in that there was no pain that I could suffer equal to the sorrow I felt when seeing him in pain.   (17:1,2,6)

*   *   *

PRAYER
> *Jesus,*
> *may I contemplate in silence*
> *this thirst,*
> *this dying,*
> *this last agony of yours.*
> *And wherever I can relieve suffering*
> *even if only by giving a cup of cold water,*
> *may I do so lovingly and willingly,*
> *knowing that this is done for you.   Amen*

Thirteenth Station

Jesus is taken down from the Cross

Since it was the day of Preparation, the Jews did not want the
bodies left on the cross during the Sabbath, especially
because the Sabbath was a day of great solemnity. So they
asked Pilate to have the legs of the crucified men broken and
the bodies removed.

Then the soldiers came and broke the legs of the first and of
the other who had been crucified with him. But when they
came to Jesus and saw that he was already dead, they did not
break his legs.

Instead, one of the soldiers pierced his side with a spear, and
at once blood and water came out. (He who saw this has
testified so that you also may believe. His testimony is true
and he knows that he tells the truth).

These things occurred so that the scripture might be fulfilled,
'None of his bones shall be broken'. And again another
passage says, 'They will look on the one whom they have
pierced'.   *(Jn.19:31-37)*

What must Mary have felt
when the dead body of Jesus
was placed in her waiting arms?
What must it have been for her
to caress the nail marks,
the bruised and lacerated skin,
to see the sightless eyes,
the pierced side still sticky with its effluviants?

Mary is every woman
who has cradled a beloved body
after an agonising death has been undergone.
She is the Rwandan or Bosnian mother
standing in the midst of a carnage
that has robbed her of husband and children.
She is the wife of one of the political detainees
of Africa or South America,
crouching by the newly discovered mass grave,
scrabbling frantically for a few bones
to cherish and bury.

She is the bewildered woman
called to her dying father's bedside,
arriving at that moment
when the last gasp breaks the shuddering silence,
while all around, the impersonal machines
of technical medicine grind to a halt.

Mary watches and grieves
as Jesus is detached from the wood.
Like the paschal lamb
his bones are unbroken,
but his pierced heart speaks of his outpoured love
more eloquently than any words.
His sufferings are over,
for that Mary is thankful.
And yet if she, and we, could but see it,
this is the moment of salvation accomplished.

Mary has remained with Jesus
through the hours of the passion.
And as he is now with the Father
so will she be
when her own hour comes.

So, for Julian,
Jesus gazes at his opened side with joy.
He has proved his love
by going to the uttermost point of life—
which is death.
He has given himself without counting the cost.

Mary's sorrow too will turn into joy,
and so will ours;
for ultimately 'all shall be well'.

*　　*　　*

I watched with all my might to see the moment when Christ
would expire and I thought I would see the body now completely dead; but I saw that it was not like that. And just at

the moment when it seemed to me that his life could not last much longer and that the end must surely be near, then suddenly, while I was looking at the crucifix as before, he changed the appearance of his blessed face. The change of his blessed face changed mine also and I felt glad and joyful to the highest degree possible.

Then our Lord gently brought to my mind: 'Where has all your pain and anguish gone to now?' And I was full of joy. I understood that for our Lord we are now with him on the cross in our pains, and that in our suffering we are dying, and with his help and grace we willingly remain on the cross until the last moment.

Suddenly we shall see the expression on his face change and then we shall be with him in heaven. Between the one and the other there shall be no lapse of time—all shall be transformed into joy. And this is what he meant when he said to me 'Where is all your pain and all your suffering now?' Thus we shall be full of happiness.

Here I saw truly that if he were to show us his blessed face now there would be no pain on earth or in any other place that could trouble us, but all would be joy and bliss for us. But because he shows his face of suffering while he carried his cross in this life, therefore we suffer pain and turmoil with him as our nature demands.

And the reason that he suffered is because he wants to make us, out of his goodness, heirs with him in joy. Moreover, as an exchange for the little pains we suffer in this life we shall have a sublime and eternal knowledge of God which we could never have had otherwise. And the harder our pains have been with him on the cross, the greater will our glory be with him in his kingdom.   *(Ch.21)*

It is God's will that we truly delight with him in our salvation, and through this he wants us to be mightily comforted and strengthened. Thus he wants our soul to be joyfully occupied with the help of his grace. For we are his bliss because in us he delights without end, and so shall we in him, with his grace. All that he does for us, has done and ever shall do, was never a cost or burden for him, nor can it be, except for the dying in our humanity, beginning at the sweet Incarnation and lasting until the blessed Rising on Easter morning. For that length of time did the cost and burden endured for our redemption last, and in this deed he rejoices endlessly.   *(23:3)*

With a joyful expression our Lord looked at his wounded side and contemplated it with joy. And with his sweet gaze he led this creature through the same wound into his side, right inside it. And there he showed me a beautiful and enjoyable place, big enough to contain all humankind that shall be saved, that they might rest there in peace and love. And with this he brought to my mind his priceless blood and the precious water which he allowed to flow out for love of us. And with this our good Lord said most blissfully: 'See how much I love you'. It was as if he said 'My dear one, behold and see your Lord, your God, who is your creator and your endless joy. See your own brother, your Saviour. My child, behold and see what delight and bliss I have in your salvation and for my love rejoice now with me.'   *(24:1a,2)*

*   *   *

PRAYER
>*Jesus,*
>*help me to truly believe*
>*that your heart was opened*
>*for each and every one of us.*
>*In you there is room for all*
>*to be cherished and loved,*
>*just as you loved and cherished your mother*
>*no matter what it must have seemed like to her*
>*when she held you after the crucifixion.*
>*Give me a spirit of faith like hers,*
>*a faith that sees beneath appearances*
>*and so is ready to let you go*
>*in order to find you again*
>*in ever new and deeper ways.   Amen*

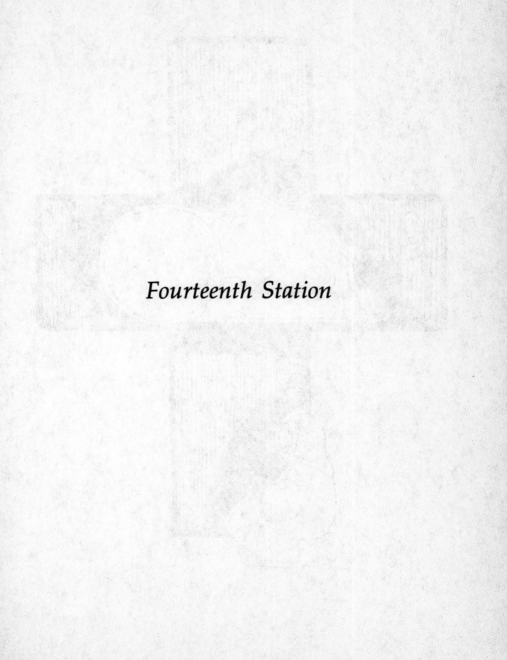

Fourteenth Station

FOURTEENTH STATION

Jesus is laid in the Sepulchre

Now there was a good and righteous man named Joseph,
who, though a member of the council, had not agreed to their
plan and action. He came from the Jewish town of Arimathea,
and he was waiting expectantly for the kingdom of God.
This man went to Pilate and asked for the body of Jesus. Then
he took it down, wrapped it in a linen cloth, and laid it in a
rock hewn tomb where no one had ever been laid.
It was the day of Preparation, and the Sabbath was beginning.
The women who had come with him from Galilee followed,
and they saw the tomb and how his body was laid. Then they
returned, and prepared spices and ointments. On the Sabbath
they rested according to the commandment.   *(Lk. 23:50-56)*

Now is the time of silence,
of waiting,
of expectancy.
We know that the end of the passion
climaxes in the Resurrection.
But it is good to pause,
to rest trustfully by the garden tomb.

It is good to share in the repose of Jesus.
His sufferings are over;
he is with the Father
and he takes us with him.
Having suffered for us
he knows only peace and joy.
In the face of such love
how can we continue to doubt.

Julian's whole life
was a living of holy Saturday,
secure in the knowledge of the Resurrection
even while her body was confined to her anchorhold.
But there is another insight of hers
which is worth pondering.
Even now, Jesus still thinks of us,

still longs for us,
until we are with him in bliss.
His joy will not be complete
until the end of the world
when he has brought all humankind
into the happiness of his kingdom.

Even though Jesus lies buried
in the darkness of the tomb,
life is still pulsing within,
bursting with longing to overwhelm the world.
Just as so much lies dormant
within our own hearts and lives,
waiting to be summoned by the touch of God
to life and fruition.

Let us with Julian
contemplate the Christ who has suffered
and the love with which
he gave himself for our sake.
If we do this
all fear will vanish
and we will want only to respond
by giving love for love
while life is still ours.

*   *   *

Our good Lord asked me; 'Are you well satisfied that I suffered for you?' I said: 'Yes good Lord, and I thank you very
much; yes good Lord, may you be blessed'. Then Jesus our
good Lord said: 'If you are satisfied, I am satisfied. To have
ever suffered the passion for you is for me a great joy, a bliss,
an endless delight. And if I could suffer more I would do so'.
And in these words: 'If I could suffer more I would do so' I
saw truly that as often as he could die he would die, and love
would never let him rest until he had done it. And I contemplated with great diligence to see how often he would have
died if he could have. And truly the number of times went
beyond my understanding and my intelligence so totally that

my reason was quite unable to comprehend or understand it.
And even if he had died or would have wanted to die so
many times, even then he would have counted that all as
nothing out of love. For he considers everything as little com-
pared to his love. Indeed, although the sweet humanity of
Christ can suffer only once, his goodness would never stop
this offering of himself. Every day he is ready to do the same
if it were possible. For if he said that for love of me he would
create new heavens and new earths, that would still be small
in comparison, for he could do this every day if he wanted to
without difficulty. But to die out of love for me so many times
that the number surpasses human reckoning, that is the
greatest offer that our Lord God could make to the human
soul, as I see it.

Now then, what he wants to say is this: 'Why then should I
not do for love of you all that I can? Death does not grieve
me, for out of love for you I would die as many times as I
could, paying no heed to the atrocious sufferings'. And this
I saw as the second way of contemplating his passion. The
love that made him suffer it surpasses all pains of his, as
much as the heaven is above the earth. For the suffering was
a noble, precious and glorious deed, accomplished once in
time by the working of love.

And the love was without beginning, is and shall be without
end. And regarding this love he said very sweetly these
words: 'If I could suffer more I would suffer more'. He did
not say 'If it were necessary to suffer more' but 'If I could
suffer more'. For even if it were not necessary and he could
suffer more he would do it. This deed and work regarding
our salvation was prepared by God with due excellence. It
was accomplished with all the dignity that Christ was capable
of. And here I saw complete joy in Christ, for his joy would
not have been complete if what has been done could have
been done in a better way.   *(22:1,4-7)*

In so far as Christ is our head he is glorified and incapable of
suffering. But concerning his body (in which all his members
are knit together) he is not yet fully glorified nor completely
beyond suffering. Therefore the same thirst and the same
longing that he experienced on the cross, that is, the desire,

longing and thirst which, as I see it, were in him from the beginning, he has them still and will have them until the last soul that shall be saved has come up into his bliss.

For as truly as there is in God the attribute of compassion and pity, so truly is there in God the attribute of thirst and longing. And by the power of this longing we too must long for him, without which no soul comes to heaven. And this attribute of longing and thirst comes from the endless goodness of God just as the attribute of pity comes from his goodness. And although he has both longing and pity these are two different attributes (as I see it) and in this consists the characteristic of the spiritual thirst which will last in him as long as we are in need, drawing us up into endless bliss.

All this was seen as a revelation of compassion, for it shall cease on Judgement Day. So he has pity and compassion for us and he desires to have us with him, but his wisdom and his love do not allow the end to come until the time is right. (31:5-7)

*   *   *

PRAYER

> *Jesus,*
> *I have come to the end*
> *of pondering with Julian on the way of the cross.*
> *But I can never exhaust the meaning*
> *contained in it,*
> *because the meaning is love*
> *and love is too deep to fathom.*
> *Thank you for your passion,*
> *thank you for your pain.*
> *May I never cease trusting*
> *in your love and mercy*
> *until the blessed day*
> *when I see you face to face in glory.   Amen*

EPILOGUE

He is
Risen

ALLELUIA

EPILOGUE

From the time I first had these revelations I often longed to know what our Lord meant. More than fifteen years later I was given in response a spiritual understanding and I was told 'Do you want to know what our Lord meant in all this? Know it well: Love was his meaning. Who showed it to you? Love. What did he show you? Love. Why did he show it to you? For love. Remain firm in this love and you will taste of it ever more deeply, for you will never know anything else from it for ever and ever.'

So I was taught that Love was what our Lord meant. And I saw very certainly that before God made us he loved us, and that this love never slackened nor ever will. In this love he has done all his works, in this love he has made all things for our benefit, and in this love our life is everlasting. In our creation we had a beginning, but the love in which he created us was in him for ever and without beginning. In this love we have our beginning. And all this we shall see in God without end.   *(86:3,4)*

Index of Bible quotations

OLD TESTAMENT

Isaiah
	page
50. 6	43
53. 4, 5	25

Lamentations
1. 12, 16	31
3. 13-17	49
3. 26-33	61

NEW TESTAMENT

Mark
15. 15	13
15. 16-20	19
15. 21	37
15. 22, 23, 25-27	73

Luke
23. 27-31	55
23. 34	73
23. 47, 48	79
23. 50-56	91

John
19. 23, 24	67
19. 28-30	79
19. 31-37	85

Galatians
| 6. 2 | 37 |

cf 1 John
| 4. 10 | 80 |

Index of Readings
from *Revelations of Divine Love*

Chapter	page	Chapter	page
2: v.1	8	27: 1, 3	28
3: 6	3	28: 1-3	39
4: 1, 2	3	31: 5-7	94
4: 4	33	37: 2	51
5: 1, 4, 5	69	38: 1	51
5: 4	10	39: 2-4	51
6: 2, 3	70	41: 5	52
7: 2, 5, 7	21	47: 2	62
8: 1-3	5	48: 3	63
8: 6	9	49: 1-3	16
9: 1	40	51: 27, 29	14
10: 2	46	52: 2, 3	63
11: 3-6	57	52: 8, 9	64
12: 2, 3	75	57: 5	34
15: 1-4	27	62: 1	40
16	81	63: 3-7	76
17: 1, 2, 6	82	71: 3-5	46
18: 1	33	72: 3-6	58
19: 1-3	10	73: 2, 3, 5-7	22
20: 1-3	15	76: 2, 4	22
21	87	78: 4, 5	28
22: 1, 4-7	93	79: 5	64
23: 3	88	86: 3, 4	97
24: 1a, 2	88	101: 5, 6	45
25: 1, 2	34		

ALSO PUBLISHED BY
THE CANTERBURY PRESS NORWICH

Margery Kempe of Lynn
and Medieval England

BY MARGARET GALLYON

Illustrated   pp. xii + pp. 226
ISBN 1-85311-111-2   £9.95